**REMARKABLE**

**PEOPLE**

# Nelson Mandela

## by Simon Rose

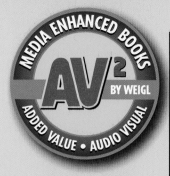

## BOOK CODE

R319667

**AV² by Weigl** brings you media enhanced books that support active learning.

AV² provides enriched content that supplements and complements this book. Weigl's AV² books strive to create inspired learning and engage young minds for a total learning experience.

Go to **www.av2books.com**, and enter this book's unique code. You will have access to video, audio, web links, quizzes, a slide show, and activities.

### Audio
Listen to sections of the book read aloud.

### Video
Watch informative video clips.

### Web Link
Find research sites and play interactive games.

### Try This!
Complete activities and hands-on experiments.

Due to the dynamic nature of the Internet, some of the URLs and activities provided as part of AV² by Weigl may have changed or ceased to exist. AV² by Weigl accepts no responsibility for any such changes. All media enhanced books are regularly monitored to update addresses and sites in a timely manner. Contact AV² by Weigl at 1-866-649-3445 or av2books@weigl.com with any questions, comments, or feedback.

Published by AV² by Weigl
350 5th Avenue, 59th Floor
New York, NY 10118

www.av2books.com     www.weigl.com

Library of Congress Cataloging-in-Publication Data

Rose, Simon, 1961-
  Nelson Mandela / Simon Rose.
     p. cm. -- (Remarkable people)
  Includes index.
  ISBN 978-1-61690-172-1 (hardcover : alk. paper) -- ISBN 978-1-61690-173-8 (softcover : alk. paper) -- ISBN 978-1-61690-174-5 (e-book)
  1.  Mandela, Nelson, 1918---Juvenile literature. 2.  Presidents--South Africa--Biography--Juvenile literature.  I. Title.
  DT1974.R67 2010
  968.06'5092--dc22
  [B]
                              2010006160

Printed in the United States in North Mankato, Minnesota
1 2 3 4 5 6 7 8 9 0  14 13 12 11 10

052010
WEP264000

**Editor:** Heather Kissock
**Design:** Terry Paulhus

**Photograph Credits**
Weigl acknowledges Getty Images as the primary image supplier for this title.

Every reasonable effort has been made to trace ownership and to obtain permission to reprint copyright material. The publishers would be pleased to have any errors or omissions brought to their attention so that they may be corrected in subsequent printings.

# Contents

# Who Is Nelson Mandela?

Nelson Mandela became the first black president of South Africa on May 10, 1994, after spending almost 27 years in prison for his political **activism**. In the 1960s, Mandela had been a leading member of the African National Congress (ANC). This group fought against **apartheid** in South Africa. Mandela's fight for black freedom led to his imprisonment in 1964. Even in prison, Mandela was a powerful symbol of the anti-apartheid movement to people worldwide.

*"For to be free is not merely to cast off one's chains, but to live in a way that respects and enhances the freedom of others."*

After his release from prison in 1990, Mandela worked with F.W. de Klerk, South Africa's president, to end apartheid peacefully. For their efforts, the men were awarded the **Nobel Peace Prize** in 1993. Shortly after winning this award, Mandela was **elected** to be president of South Africa. He stayed in this position until his retirement in 1999.

Nelson Mandela has always believed in a free society where people live together in harmony. His struggle to end apartheid remains an inspiration for millions of people. In November 2009, the United Nations announced that July 18, Mandela's birthday, is to be known as "Mandela Day." This day honors Mandela's contribution to freedom around the world.

# Growing Up

Nelson Mandela was born in the Transkei region of South Africa on July 18, 1918. His birth name was Rolihlahla. Nelson's father, Henry Mgadla Mandela, was the chief of the local town. His mother, Nonqaphi Nosekeni, was the chief's third wife. Nelson was one of 13 children. When he was nine years old, his father died.

Nelson was the first member of his family to go to school. He first attended school at a local mission. In 1937, he moved to Healdtown to attend high school. After graduation, Mandela began studying at the University of Fort Hare. This was a top school for black Africans. Many students from Fort Hare went on to play leading roles in the **independence** struggles of a number of African countries. At Fort Hare, Mandela met Oliver Tambo. The two became lifelong friends and colleagues.

■ Mandela was given his English name when he started school. One of his teachers named him "Nelson."

# Get to Know South Africa

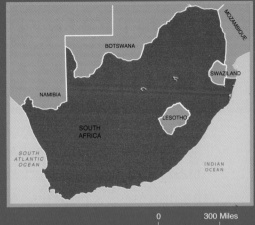

**ANIMAL**
Springbok

**FLAG**

**BIRD**
Blue Crane

0 ——— 300 Miles
0 ——— 300 Kilometers

The population of South Africa is about 49 million.

The country has 11 official languages and several unofficial ones.

In 2010, South Africa became the first African country to host the World Cup of soccer.

South Africa is south of the equator. The country has its summer when it is winter in North America.

South Africa has many protected wildlife and marine areas, including Kruger National Park.

South Africa is home to many cultures and languages. How do you think growing up in South Africa affected Nelson Mandela's personal and political beliefs? Research the area where you live. How have the cultures of all the people living there enriched your part of the world?

# Practice Makes Perfect

During his first year at the University of Fort Hare, Mandela became involved in a student **boycott**. The students were protesting against the university's **policies**. As a result, Mandela was expelled from the university. He moved to Johannesburg. There, he completed his degree by correspondence through the University of South Africa. At the same time, Mandela was working as a clerk at a law firm. Mandela then studied law at the University of Witwatersrand. In 1944, he joined the ANC.

In 1948, the National Party was elected to form the government of South Africa. This party began the policy of apartheid. By this time, Mandela had been elected as secretary to the youth leadership of the ANC. The ANC Youth Leadership (ANCYL) worked toward gaining **citizenship** and voting rights for all South Africans, regardless of **race**.

■ After Mandela completed his schooling, he opened a law firm with Oliver Tambo. The firm provided low-cost legal services to black people.

Mandela became a main figure in the ANC. In 1952, he was arrested for protesting against apartheid. He also took part in a conference called the Congress of the People in 1955. At this event, the Freedom Charter was adopted. Many of the charter's demands were written into the South African **constitution** decades later.

During a peaceful protest in December 1956, Mandela and about 150 others were arrested and charged with **treason**. They were accused of trying to overthrow the South African government. Their legal fight became known as the Treason Trial. It lasted until 1961. All those who were arrested were set free.

■ In 2007, Mandela was given a book of newspaper clippings from the Treason Trial. The woman who gave them to him was the daughter of the judge at the trial.

While the Treason Trial was taking place, the Sharpeville Massacre occurred. Police opened fire on a crowd of people protesting South Africa's **pass laws**. Sixty-nine people were killed, and more than 180 were wounded. The Sharpeville Massacre led to the banning of the ANC and other anti-apartheid groups.

After the shooting, the ANC founded a military group called Spear of the Nation. Mandela was named the group's commander. He had always supported non-violent protest. However, he knew that a stronger stance had to be taken in the struggle for black equality. He began campaigning against the government and military. Mandela also left the country illegally. He spoke at conferences and met with other African governments. When Mandela returned to South Africa, he was arrested for leaving the country and sentenced to five years in prison.

■ At Sharpeville, the police attempted to disperse the protestors by flying jets low over the crowd. When this failed, they opened fire.

# Thoughts from Mandela

Nelson Mandela is a champion for the rights and freedoms of people all over the world. Here are some of the statements he has made about his beliefs and the lessons he has learned in his fight for equality.

**Mandela speaks about the struggles that occur when fighting for freedom.**

"There is no easy walk to freedom anywhere, and many of us will have to pass through the valley of the shadow of death again and again before we reach the mountaintops of our desires."

**Mandela refuses to be freed from prison if he has to support apartheid.**

"Only free men can negotiate; prisoners cannot enter into contracts."

**Mandela shows his respect for democracy.**

"During my lifetime I have dedicated myself to this struggle of the African people. ... I have cherished the ideal of a democratic and free society in which all persons live together in harmony and with equal opportunities."

**Mandela discusses the lessons he has learned about courage.**

"I learned that courage was not the absence of fear, but the triumph over it. The brave man is not he who does not feel afraid, but he who conquers that fear."

**Mandela states his views on racism.**

"I detest racialism, ...whether it comes from a black man or a white man."

**Mandela talks about how to make peace.**

"If you want to make peace with your enemy, you have to work with your enemy. Then he becomes your partner."

# What was Apartheid?

Apartheid means "apartness" in **Afrikaans**. It was a system of separating people by race. Apartheid was adopted by the South African government in 1948. It remained in place until 1994.

Apartheid laws ensured white people had better treatment than black people in schools, hospitals, and other public services. Black people were forced from their homes because certain areas were for whites only.

Black people had been denied the right to vote in 1936. In 1959, many also lost their South African citizenship. They instead became citizens of one of the 10 "homelands." These were areas where black people were forced to live. Black people had to carry a "pass book" if they traveled outside their homeland. The book had information, photographs, and fingerprints of the person.

■ Anti-apartheid supporters often called for the release of all the political prisoners in South Africa.

# Apartheid 101

## Hendrick Verwoerd (1901–1966)

Hendrick Verwoerd made many Apartheid policies during the early 1950s as South Africa's Minister of Native Affairs. When Verwoerd became prime minister in 1958, he played a key role in changing the country's politics. Under his watch, the country became a **republic**. The African National Congress was banned. Nelson Mandela and other anti-apartheid activists were jailed. Hendrick Verwoerd was killed by an assassin in Cape Town, South Africa, in 1966.

## Frederick Willem de Klerk (1936– )

F. W. de Klerk was the last State President of South Africa in the apartheid period from 1989 to 1994. De Klerk was responsible for releasing Mandela from prison in 1990. This marked the beginning of the end of apartheid. De Klerk worked to make South Africa a place where all people had equal rights. De Klerk and Mandela shared the Nobel Peace Prize in 1993.

## Pieter Willem Botha (1916–2006)

P. W. Botha became president of South Africa in 1978. He made small changes to the apartheid system. However, he failed to make the changes that were needed to truly change the country. He fell from power in 1989.

## Desmond Tutu (1931– )

Desmond Tutu was the first black South African Anglican Bishop of Cape Town. He became known around the world as one of the leading people against apartheid in the 1980s. Tutu was awarded the Nobel Peace Prize in 1984. Mandela made Tutu chairman of the Truth and Reconciliation Commission. This group researched human rights during apartheid.

### Racism

Racism is the belief that a certain ethnic group is better than another. Many governments, including South Africa and the United States, have separated people by race at certain times. Some ethnic groups are denied certain rights or benefits.

# Influences

**M**artin Luther King, Jr. was an American civil rights leader. He believed in non-violent protest. King fought for African American civil rights in the United States in the 1950s and 1960s. Like Mandela, King was awarded the Nobel Peace Prize. He received the award in 1964 for his work to end racial **segregation** and **discrimination**. King's work was similar to Mandela's work in South Africa.

Mahatma Gandhi was a great influence on Mandela. Gandhi is known as the non-violent leader of India's fight for independence. He held protests and demonstrations against British rule from the 1920s until 1948. Gandhi's methods of non-violent protest were known as *satyagraha*. This means "insistence on truth."

■ Mahatma Gandhi lived in South Africa for 20 years. Many of these years were spent fighting discrimination.

Mandela agreed with Gandhi's views on non-violent protest. In January 2007, Mandela attended a conference in New Delhi, India. The event marked 100 years since Gandhi introduced satyagraha to South Africa.

## STEPHEN BIKO

Stephen Biko was a South African anti-apartheid activist in the 1960s and 1970s. He first became involved in politics as a student leader. Biko was the founder of the Black Consciousness Movement. This was a political movement that took place in the mid-1960s. It replaced the banned African National Congress. Biko died in police custody due to mistreatment.

■ Following Biko's death, people gathered to protest the treatment he received while in custody.

# Overcoming Obstacles

While serving his five-year prison sentence, Mandela was charged with another crime. He was accused of treason for his role in planning campaigns against the government. This time, Mandela was sentenced to life in prison.

Mandela was first held in a prison on Robben Island. It was located off the coast from Cape Town. Conditions in prison were harsh. Prisoners had a small cell with a thin mat for a bed and a bucket for a toilet. Black prisoners received the least food. **Political prisoners**, like Mandela, had almost no rights. He was allowed just one visitor and one letter every six months.

■ Mandela's prison cell was about 21.5 square feet (2 square meters) in size.

In 1982, Mandela was moved to Pollsmoor Prison on the South Africa mainland. Some people believe he held secret meetings there with the South African government. In 1985, South African President P. W. Botha offered to release Mandela from prison. Mandela had to promise to give up his fight against apartheid. He refused.

While Mandela was in prison, he became known all over the world as South Africa's most important black leader. People across the globe demanded his freedom. In 1988, Mandela was moved to Victor Verster Prison. There, he lived in a private house. President F. W. de Klerk ordered his release in February 1990.

■ When he left prison, Mandela and then-wife Winnie saluted a cheering crowd of supporters.

# Achievements and Successes

In 1990, the South African government took the first major steps to end apartheid. That year, the government removed the ban on anti-apartheid groups. This included the ANC. It also released Mandela from prison. Mandela then worked closely with President F. W. de Klerk to end apartheid in South Africa. In 1993, both men were jointly awarded the Nobel Peace Prize for their work toward equal rights for all people in South Africa.

In 1994, Mandela became the first black president of South Africa. He was to serve a five-year term. During his term, a new constitution was to be created for the country.

■ Supporters gathered to cheer for Mandela throughout the 1994 election campaign.

Nelson Mandela retired in 1999, but he did not stop working. He continued to work for a peaceful end to conflicts in other parts of Africa. Mandela has helped work toward HIV/AIDS awareness, as well as to improve South Africa's reputation around the world. He also helped South Africa secure the 2010 soccer World Cup.

Mandela retired from public life in 2004. He decided to spend more time with his family and friends. Today, millions of people around the world continue to be inspired by his efforts to create a free society.

## INVICTUS

The 2009 movie *Invictus* tells the story of an experience early in Mandela's presidency. The country was in the process of moving beyond apartheid. Mandela needed to find a cause that would join all South Africans. He believed the country's rugby team, the Springboks, could help achieve his goal. Even though the team was not likely to win the World Cup, Mandela encouraged them to play hard for their country. The team worked hard and won the World Cup. The country came together in victory.

■ Morgan Freeman played the role of Nelson Mandela in the movie *Invictus*.

# Write a Biography

A person's life story can be the subject of a book. This kind of book is called a biography. Biographies describe the lives of remarkable people, such as those who have achieved great success or have done important things to help others. These people may be alive today, or they may have lived many years ago. Reading a biography can help you learn more about a remarkable person.

At school you might be asked to write a biography. First, decide whom you want to write about. You can choose a political activist, such as Nelson Mandela, or any other person you find interesting. Then, find out if your library has any books about this person. Learn as much as you can about him or her. Write down the key events in the person's life. What was this person's childhood like? What has he or she accomplished? What are his or her goals? What makes this person special or unusual?

A concept web is a useful research tool. Read the questions in the following concept web. Answer the questions in your notebook. Your answers will help you write your biography.

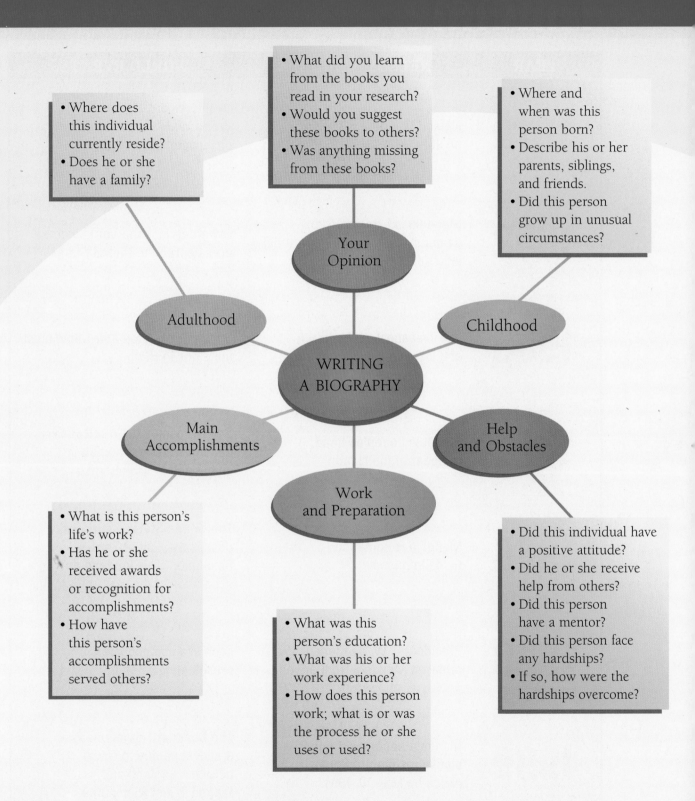

- Where does this individual currently reside?
- Does he or she have a family?

- What did you learn from the books you read in your research?
- Would you suggest these books to others?
- Was anything missing from these books?

- Where and when was this person born?
- Describe his or her parents, siblings, and friends.
- Did this person grow up in unusual circumstances?

Your Opinion

Adulthood

Childhood

WRITING A BIOGRAPHY

Main Accomplishments

Help and Obstacles

Work and Preparation

- What is this person's life's work?
- Has he or she received awards or recognition for accomplishments?
- How have this person's accomplishments served others?

- What was this person's education?
- What was his or her work experience?
- How does this person work; what is or was the process he or she uses or used?

- Did this individual have a positive attitude?
- Did he or she receive help from others?
- Did this person have a mentor?
- Did this person face any hardships?
- If so, how were the hardships overcome?

# Timeline

| YEAR | NELSON MANDELA | WORLD EVENTS |
|------|----------------|--------------|
| 1918 | Nelson Mandela is born on July 18, 1918. | World War I comes to an end on November 11, 1918. |
| 1952 | Mandela is arrested for demonstrating against apartheid with other ANC members. | Dwight D. Eisenhower is elected president of the United States. |
| 1956 | The Treason Trial begins and lasts until 1961. | Soviet troops stop anti-Communist uprisings in Hungary. |
| 1961 | Mandela becomes head of Spear of the Nation. | Soviet cosmonaut Yuri Gagarin becomes the first human in space and to orbit Earth. |
| 1964 | Mandela is sentenced to life in prison. | The United States Congress passes the Gulf of Tonkin Resolution. This leads to an escalation of the war in Vietnam. |
| 1990 | President F. W. de Klerk releases Mandela from prison. | Lech Walesa becomes president of Poland. |
| 1999 | Mandela becomes the first black president of South Africa on May 10, 1994. | The Channel Tunnel opens. It allows people to travel between England and France in just 35 minutes. |

**activism:** action taken to achieve political goals

**Afrikaans:** the main language of the white rulers of South Africa

**apartheid:** meaning "separateness" in Afrikaans, this was a system of racial segregation imposed by the government until 1994

**boycott:** to stop using something as a form of protest

**citizenship:** having rights and responsibilities as a resident of a country

**civil rights:** the basic rights guaranteed to the citizens of a country

**constitution:** a document that details the laws of a country

**democracy:** a government in which every adult citizen of a country has the right to vote and elect representatives to an assembly

**discrimination:** treating a person unfairly because of his or her race, gender, age, or physical or mental condition

**elected:** chosen by the people in a majority vote

**independence:** not influenced or controlled by others

**Nobel Peace Prize:** an international prize to recognize the person, people, or groups who work toward world peace

**pass laws:** laws that kept Black South Africans from moving freely within the country

**policies:** rules and standards

**political prisoners:** people put in prison for their political beliefs or acts

**race:** a grouping of people based mainly on physical features

**republic:** a country that does not have a king or queen as its head of government

**segregation:** having separate services and facilities for people of different races

**treason:** the act of trying to overthrow the government

# Log on to www.av2books.com

AV[2] by Weigl brings you media enhanced books that support active learning. Go to **www.av2books.com**, and enter the special code inside the front cover of this book. You will gain access to enriched and enhanced content that supplements and complements this book. Content includes video, audio, web links, quizzes, a slide show, and activities.

**Audio**
Listen to sections of the book read aloud.

**Video**
Watch informative video clips.

**Web Link**
Find research sites and play interactive games.

**Try This!**
Complete activities and hands-on experiments.

# WHAT'S ONLINE?

| Try This! Complete activities and hands-on experiments. | Web Link Find research sites and play interactive games. | Video Watch informative video clips. | EXTRA FEATURES |
|---|---|---|---|
| **Pages 6-7** Complete an activity about your childhood. | **Pages 8-9** Learn more about Nelson Mandela's life. | **Pages 4-5** Watch a video about Nelson Mandela. | **Audio** Hear introductory audio at the top of every page |
| **Pages 10-11** Try this activity about key events. | **Pages 14-15** Find out more about the people who influenced Nelson Mandela. | **Pages 12-13** Check out a video about Nelson Mandela. | **Key Words** Study vocabulary, and play a matching word game. |
| **Pages 16-17** Complete an activity about overcoming obstacles. | **Pages 18-19** Learn more about Nelson Mandela's achievements. | | **Slide Show** View images and captions, and try a writing activity. |
| **Pages 20-21** Write a biography. | **Pages 20-21** Check out this site about Nelson Mandela. | | **AV[2] Quiz** Take this quiz to test your knowledge |
| **Page 22** Try this timeline activity. | | | |